FX!

Costumes and Makeup

Hocking County
District Library
West Main Street
Logan, Ohio 43138

Jessica Larson
and Karen Larson

Consultants

Timothy Rasinski, Ph.D.
Kent State University

Lori Oczkus, M.A.
Literacy Consultant

Publishing Credits

Rachelle Cracchiolo, M.S.Ed., *Publisher*
Conni Medina, M.A.Ed., *Managing Editor*
Dona Herweck Rice, *Series Developer*
Emily R. Smith, M.A.Ed., *Content Director*
Stephanie Bernard/Susan Daddis, M.A.Ed., *Editors*
Robin Erickson, *Senior Graphic Designer*

The TIME logo is a registered trademark of TIME Inc. Used under license.

Image Credits: Cover and p.1 Monika Skolimowska/EPA/Newscom; p.8 Kobby Dagan/Shutterstock.com; p.9 (top) SEEK REPLACEMENT; p.10 Daily Mail/Rex/Alamy Stock Photo; p.11 Onur Coban/Anadolu Agency/Getty Images; p.12 Xavier Zimbardo/Getty Images; p.14 BJI/Blue Jean Images/Getty Images; p.16 NEED PERMISSIONS; pp.28–29 NEED PERMISSIONS; p.32 Joan Marcus; p.34 SEE ALT; p.39 Michel Dufour/WireImage/Getty Images; p.40 Blue Jean Images/Alamy Stock Photo; p.42 Carlo Allegri/Getty Images; p.50 20th Century Fox/United Archives GmbH/Alamy Stock Photo; p.51 Anne-Marie Jackson/Toronto Star via Getty Images; p.55 Walt Disney Pictures/AF archive/Alamy Stock Photo; p.56 GREG RYAN/Alamy Stock Photo; all other images from iStock and/or Shutterstock.

Teacher Created Materials

5301 Oceanus Drive
Huntington Beach, CA 92649-1030
http://www.tcmpub.com

ISBN 978-1-4938-3613-0
© 2017 Teacher Created Materials, Inc.

Table of Contents

Behind the Curtain

"Costumes are the first impression that you have of the character."—Colleen Atwood (Academy Award®-winning costume designer)

When you join a theater audience, you are invited into a new world. The lights are dimmed, the stage is set, and the actors deliver their performances. On stage, there are always invisible hands at play—**artisans** who have done their work long before the actors say their first lines. These talented people help you to fall fully into the world of the play with their precise hands, careful research, and creative ideas.

Costume designers and makeup artists have the exciting task of bringing characters to life. The costumes give audiences a better sense of who the characters are. Similarly, makeup artists transform actors into glamorous characters or hideous creatures.

Now, picture a scene from your favorite play. How do the costumes and makeup help convey the story? In what ways do the costume designers' and makeup artists' choices **enhance** your understanding of the characters?

Step behind the curtain to discover how costumes are created from start to finish and how makeup enhances the characters and storyline.

In the Spotlight

The Phantom of the Opera is the longest-running Broadway show with more than 11,000 performances. Stage costumes need to be able to endure long performance runs and quick changes. Designers must keep this in mind when crafting a costume for the stage.

Lights! Camera! Action!

With the introduction of film came the close-up. Costume pieces in movies have to be much more detailed and historically accurate to maintain the **suspension of disbelief** for the movie-going audience.

Costuming History

Theatrical performances date back to the ancient Greeks in 700 BC. Theater (also spelled *theatre*) comes from the Greek word *theatron*, meaning "a place for viewing." They developed out of religious **rituals**. Each town had an outdoor theater, and thousands of people showed up for performances. All actors were men, and the costumes were everyday clothing. The audience would know the character's gender, age, and even social status by the clothes he wore. Costumes and masks have played an important part of the storytelling process ever since.

Ancient Greek Theater

Ancient Greek Theater

Knee-length **tunics** were worn for male characters, while female characters wore longer robes with pieces of cloth draped over their shoulders. When playing women, men wore **body stockings** designed to imitate the female figure. Each performer dressed for his part. Actors playing strangers wore colorful costumes, tragic characters wore tall boots, high-class characters wore platform shoes, and comedic actors wore plain socks.

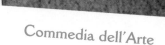

Commedia Dell'Arte

Commedia dell'Arte

In sixteenth century Italy, **commedia dell'arte** was in full swing. There were six types of characters in this theatrical style, and each character had its own mask and costume. The masks had very strong **features**, such as pointy noses, thin mustaches, or plump lips. The costumes, like those of the Greeks, told about the characters' social statuses and personalities.

Masks in Theater

The comedy and tragedy masks we associate with theater came from Greek mythology. Japanese *Noh* drama uses painted and carved wood masks to portray 60 different characters. During the Renaissance, performers wore masks to entertain the royal court. Masks continue to be used in modern theater and throughout world cultures.

Kabuki Theater

Kabuki Theater

Kabuki theater began in Japan in the seventeenth century with women performing all roles. In later years, male actors took over. They wore face makeup and costumes specific to their character types. The colors and lines on an actor's painted face tell the audience who he is. The face, neck, and hands are painted white with red lines around the eyes and lips. Other colored lines are added if the character is a villain or a hero. Each character also has a special type of wig. Traditional **embroidered** silk kimonos with an **obi** are worn with long pants that trail behind the actors.

No Sweat

Most Kabuki costumes are thrown away after the run of the play because the actors' sweat has ruined them.

Elizabethan Theater

Elizabethan Theater

In Elizabethan times (1558–1603), only men acted in plays. A costume for a female character included a **corset**, stockings, **pantalets** and underskirt, a gown, a full skirt dress, a high collar, and tie-on sleeves. A male character wore a shirt, stockings, a corset, **britches**, a well-fitted coat with tie-on sleeves, a high collar, a **cravat**, an overcoat, a cape, and a hat. The costume usually weighed more than the person who wore it! Makeup of a white face, red cheeks, and a blonde wig would turn a boy actor into a young woman. If two characters wore the same makeup and wig, they were twins!

To Be or Not To Be

William Shakespeare was first an actor and then a playwright during Elizabethan times. His many histories, tragedies, and comedies are still performed all over the world.

Designing for Realism

Designing for Realism

Costume design for **realism** may sound easy. The characters are often ordinary people acting out real-life situations. But the clothing needs to stay true to that time period. To do that, the designer may look at photographs and film clips to study the styles. For example, *Hairspray!* portrays people in 1960s Baltimore. Reading the script lets the designer know the characters' ages and personalities. Drawings are then made to help the director see the designer's plans.

Bring It On!

Designers particularly love to work on challenging creations. Problem solving in a creative way is the hallmark of the designer's trade!

It is important for the costumer to explain how he or she wants the costumes to be worn and treated by actors. Additionally, the more the costume designer listens to the actors' hopes related to their costumes, the more exciting the end result is for all involved.

Fantasy Design

Fantasy Design

Fantasy creations might lead designers to look through racks of existing costumes to find inspiration. By shortening a dress, adding sleeves, or dyeing a shirt, old costumes can be given new life. But, fantasy can pose tricky challenges, too. Designing for *Shrek the Musical*, for example, means figuring out how to make Pinocchio's nose grow and building the **mechanics** into the costume. Also, Fiona's look must change from a princess to an ogre in 30 seconds!

Collaboration Is Key

Working on a theatrical production requires teamwork. The director and producers gather a creative team to develop the show. This group works together to help bring the director's vision to life. This collaboration can be fun and fulfilling.

Director's Vision

At the first **production meeting**, the creative team of directors, producers, and designers talks about the play. The director explains his or her vision for the show or film. This vision may include themes for focus, visual elements, tone, and impact on the audience. This helps designers decide how to move ahead with their work. Designers also learn important deadlines for finishing the work at these meetings. This is called the production schedule.

Presenting...the Designs!

Usually, designers think of their work as being behind the camera or curtain. But during design presentations, they actually take the stage. Through the first week of rehearsals for a professional production, the designers show all their hard work. They take turns presenting their ideas. Fabric **swatches**, color **palettes**, and **renderings** are shown to the cast and crew. When the presentations by the designers are over, the production team and cast discuss the vision of the show.

Make Your Point

In any business meeting, including a theatrical one, using technology such as PowerPoint® or Prezi® can make a design presentation more interesting. It also helps to catch the eye of the audience. Since the pictures can be projected and seen by more people at once, everyone is engaged.

Design Meetings

Designers collaborate with each other throughout the production in design meetings. When costumers work with makeup and hair designers, the end result is truly impressive. The right style of wig and makeup enhances a costume.

It also helps for the costume designer to understand the role of lighting. Clear information about the fabrics and colors being used in costumes can assist a lighting designer. Finally, talking with the set designer is key. When the set and costumes work together, the audience can get a better sense of time, place, and mood.

Time and Money

A costume designer must be organized. Planning done in the early stages helps the costumer meet the demands of the schedule. The designer must get every actor costumed before opening night. Working backward from opening night to set the schedule allows for all deadlines to be met and costumes to be ready on time.

Of course, sticking to the costume budget is essential. Costume designers need to keep a careful eye on all money spent. The costs of costume pieces, fabrics, **notions**, and rental costumes are written down and totaled. This helps to keep the production within budget.

Swatch It

Designers often use pieces of fabric to help others visualize the costume before it is made. Lighting and set designers use **gels** and paint samples in the same way. All swatches can be viewed and commented on in design meetings.

THINK LINK

⊚ What collaborative skills are required to work on a creative team?

⊚ How does the presentation of designs in the first week of rehearsals help the cast and crew of the production?

⊚ In what ways do good organizational skills help a costume designer?

Theater Questions and Answers

Creating the world of a play requires communication and dedication. The following responses are from theater professionals.

What is your favorite part of collaborating with designers?

Paul Larson, *Director:* I love to see what my designers come up with throughout the weeks leading up to the opening of the show. It's great to see how their ideas enhance the production.

How do you begin your design process?

Jeanette Ceravolo Capuano, *Costumer:* Research! I go on the Internet and see how past productions costumed and then put my spin on it.

What is the biggest designing challenge?

Melissa Hoogenraad, *Makeup Designer:* Art is never the same. The biggest challenge is not being influenced by others. As the professional artist hired to create and bring the vision to life, the vision of the director is all that matters.

What advice would you give a future designer?

Paul: Keep an open mind. There are lots of ideas out there to work with, and it's your job to shake them out. Most importantly, have fun!

Jeanette: Do your research and homework. Be ready to defend your choices. You want this to be your best work.

Melissa: Believe in yourself and create as much as you can. Know you have this creativity for a reason. Embrace it and chase your dreams while being yourself!

The "Knitty" Gritty

In costume design, it's all about the details. Sure, a designer must be aware of the big picture requirements of the production, but it's the nitty-gritty details that really bring things to life.

It's All in the Fit

Recording actors' measurements on body **templates** guides the costumer in getting the correct fit for all costume pieces. In most productions, actors have multiple costumes. For example, in *The Little Mermaid* stage production, Ariel changes between a mermaid and a human several times. She has her mermaid outfit and several human outfits. These quick changes require sturdy, well-fitted costumes.

Then, there are the actors who are cast in more than one role in the same play. The costumes, hair, and makeup can be very different for each role. Supporting actors in **touring companies** often play multiple roles. They might play a butler, a townsperson, and a sea creature all in the space of two hours! It is easy to see why getting accurate measurements is important.

Gems or Junk?

Costumes have to be well made to survive the stress of many performances. Fashionable street clothing may only be worn a few times. But in a successful stage production, a costume may be worn every night for months or even years.

Get Fit!

Hats, gloves, wigs, and other accessories must coordinate with the costumes, too, and they must fit well. An actor shouldn't have to worry about a wig slipping or a shoe falling off during a scene—unless, of course, she is playing Cinderella!

The Plot Thickens!

The costumer reads carefully through the script, scene by scene. She takes notes of what costumes are needed for all the characters. These costumes are written on a **costume plot**. The plot helps the costumer keep track of the overall look of the show. In this way, she makes sure that characters are dressed differently, with colors and styles that reflect their personalities but also work with others. The designer may also talk to the performers to get a better understanding of their characters. The actors best know the characters' emotions and movements. Using their research, notes, and conversations, the costumer sketches the costume designs.

Combing through the Racks

To find the costumes, a search is first done through costume storage. Previously used costumes can be **altered** at little cost. Hunting through thrift stores' clothing departments also may provide suitable pieces for costumes. For low-budget productions, asking the cast members for items that they may have at home is another option. The production may require specialty items that can be rented from a costume warehouse or borrowed from another studio or theater. Finally, some costumes may need to be made. This means buying fabrics, patterns, and all the notions required to construct the costumes. This option will cost the most time and money, but the costume will be exactly what the director wants!

Costuming Conundrum

One challenge in designing costumes for the Broadway show *Hamilton* was how to mix the eighteenth century setting with the modern hip-hop script. Paul Tazewell, the costume designer, decided that everything from the actors' shoulders down would reflect the time period. Necks and heads would be contemporary.

Color Palettes

To create a color palette for costume pieces, the designer needs to keep in mind the director's vision. Color palettes will bring out the emotions of the characters, the time period, and the story being told. Knowing a bit about how to combine colors will help in developing a successful palette. The red, yellow, and blue base colors of the color wheel can be divided into warm and cool colors. Blues and greens are cool colors, and yellows and reds are warm colors. The basic color wheel can be expanded with tints, shades, and tones. When creating a palette, a family of colors should be used.

Know Your Fabrics

Designers often have to shop on a budget, but making wise choices when buying fabric can make a difference. Stretchy material is less likely to tear during repeated changes. Cotton is a lighter fabric that breathes and stretches comfortably for most actors. Spandex and Lycra are common in costumes in which dancing is required. Using polyester for blends can be smart if wrinkles are a concern. Feathered and sequined fabrics are likely to shed and catch on things. Whatever the show, research will help the designer to understand which fabrics will be most appropriate.

Costume Parade

Shortly before the opening of a stage production, there will be a costume parade. All the actors walk onstage under the lights in their costumes for final notes from the director and costumer. Then, adjustments can be made.

Color Wheel

YELLOW
primary

YELLOW GREEN
tertiary

YELLOW ORANGE
tertiary

GREEN
secondary

ORANGE
secondary

BLUE GREEN
tertiary

RED ORANGE
tertiary

BLUE
primary

RED
primary

BLUE VIOLET
tertiary

RED VIOLET
tertiary

VIOLET
secondary

23

Putting It Together

The search through costume storage, **vintage** stores, and fabric bins leads the designer to discover clothing and materials that can be used in making his or her own designs come to life. Now, it's time to get started on the actual construction of the costume pieces!

The Right Stitch

Altering clothing to make it into a costume for the show or film requires some sewing skills and plenty of imagination. Decorative trim, buttons, or bows can be added by hand stitching. Cutting off sleeves or removing a ruffle on a dress will change the look. Maybe all the garment needs is to be shortened or taken in to fit properly. Or perhaps more drastic changes are needed, such as combining two pieces of clothing into one! There are as many ways to alter a piece of clothing as there are types of clothing. Adapting an already constructed piece of clothing saves time and money.

Be Thrifty!
Vintage stores aren't just a good place to find clothing. Designers may discover purses, shoes, hats, and scarves at these shops, too.

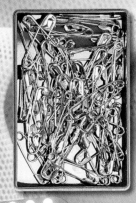

Tools of the Trade

Some costume designers keep sewing kits handy to make quick costume fixes. These kits can include double-sided tape, pre-threaded needles, a steamer, and safety pins.

Sew What?!

All students of costuming need to know basic sewing skills to create costumes. Hand stitching is used to attach buttons, snaps, and hooks. Hemstitches can be done by hand or by machine to change the length of a hem or a sleeve. Knowing how to use clothing patterns is also very important. Instructions are included in a pattern's envelope that guide the costumer on the correct amount of fabric, the layout of the pattern pieces on the fabric, and sewing the pieces together.

Most patterns require machine stitching. Knowing how to pin fabric pieces together, how to sew seams on a sewing machine, and how to use other machine stitches are musts when it comes to costuming. Another valuable sewing technique is draping. Draping is placing, pinning, and **basting** fabric on a dress form to create a costume piece. A designer can start with an idea from a sketch or can play with the fabric selected to form it into a new design. Once the fabric is pinned and tacked together, it is removed from the form. Then it is either sewn together or used to make a pattern for the costume.

Pattern This!

Suppose you find what you're looking for but it's the wrong color or size, or you need ten of them. Think about how you would adapt a garment you own.

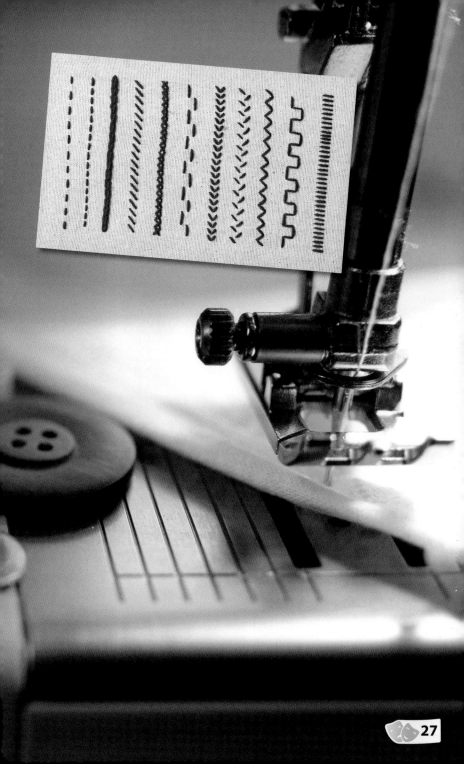

Pattern It!

Making a pattern can be as simple as tracing the pieces from clothing you already have on hand.

To do it, you will need these items:

- ◎ **1 roll of postal wrapping paper, cut into large pieces**
- ◎ **1 fabric pen**
- ◎ **1 blouse (or shirt)**
- ◎ scissors
- ◎ iron

Instructions

1. Find the middle of the neck and fold the blouse in half. Lay the blouse flat on a piece of paper.
2. Trace half the blouse on paper.
3. Fold back the sleeve at the armhole and sketch the curve.

4. Remove the blouse and draw a line 1 inch (2.5 cm) from the traced line all around. This will be the extra fabric needed for the seams.

5. Fold the pattern. Cut the pattern through both layers of the paper. Now you have the pattern for the blouse back.

6. Repeat Steps 1–5 to make the pattern for the blouse front.

7. For the sleeve, fold another piece of paper in half and place it under the blouse sleeve with the fold parallel to the top of the sleeve. Place the pattern you made on top, matching the armhole curve to your blouse. Trace the open part of the sleeve. Fold the sleeve up over the pattern and trace the armhole curve from the fold down, adding 1 inch (2.5 cm) for the seams.

8. Unfold all your patterns and iron to get rid of fold lines.

Now you are ready to put your pattern to use and make your own blouse!

Makeup History

Makeup is used nearly every day by women and men in many parts of the world. Tutorials online teach all sorts of tips for daily wear. How different is makeup for stage and screen? Some people think it's very different. Let's look into the similarities, differences, and techniques used to bring a character to life through makeup.

Foundations of Makeup

Nearly every society of the last 6,000 years has used some form of makeup. Some **archaeologists** claim that as far back as 100,000 years ago, people applied makeup during rituals in Africa. Ancient Egyptians used oils, henna, and eyeliner powder known as *kohl*. Some ancient Greeks used treatments made from lead to whiten their skin and *ochre* to redden their lips.

Women in China wore plum blossom designs on their cheeks and foreheads. In Japan, women called *geishas* adopted a distinctive look. They whitened their faces with rice powder and painted their lips bright red. They lined and shadowed their eyes with black and other colors to draw attention to them. In England, Queen Elizabeth I used lead to lighten her complexion.

Makeup trends worldwide have changed as fashion gained prominence. Films, designers, and now social media all affect beauty standards.

Dying for Beauty?

Many of the earliest beauty treatments were made of lead, mercury, and arsenic. These materials are poisonous. As the skin is the largest organ of the body, you can imagine what happened after applying these substances to it.

Queen Elizabeth I

Cleopatra: Makeup Icon

The Egyptian queen in the first century BC was well known for her power and beauty. She wore colorful liner on her eyes, darkened her eyebrows, and reddened her lips. She is also believed to have used henna to dye her nails.

Birth of Stage Makeup

Although masks dominated the early ages of theater history, one Greek actor changed that. Thespis is known as the first true actor because he played a character other than himself. He covered his face with white lead and stained his lips and cheeks with wine to highlight his features for large audiences. Through Thespis, theatrical makeup was introduced, although it would take years for it to be used widely.

Feminine Face

Men and boys were assigned to play the female parts in Shakespeare's day. The most beautiful women were said to be pale skinned with blonde hair, so makeup and wigs were essential. Actors would lighten their complexions with the toxic mixture of white lead and vinegar known as ceruse. Another mixture made of hog bones and poppy oil also became popular.

Morality Plays

In the 1500s, makeup was worn in religious plays in medieval Europe. The actors used a variety of paints and **pigments** that they mixed by hand and applied to create their characters. Actors playing God painted their faces in gold, while angels painted their faces red. Audiences could identify characters based on their makeup designs.

Art Imitates Life

During Shakespeare's time, actors **mimicked** the style of makeup of Queen Elizabeth I. Chalk, flour, or lead was used to whiten the skin. Soot from the fires was used to accentuate the eyes, and it helped actors draw on wrinkles to look old or dirty. Wool was used to create facial hair and wigs. As men would play the women's parts, they paid special attention to creating more feminine characteristics with stains for cheeks and lips.

The Roar of the Greasepaint

Theatrical makeup transformed alongside the types of plays being performed. Big performances and broad themes evolved into simpler storytelling in many parts of the world. The role of makeup also evolved as the applications advanced over time.

The 1800s brought a change in makeup application. Toxic combinations of lead and oils were replaced by a mixture of melted tallow, or lard, and pigment. These colorful, thick creams were known as greasepaint. This advancement brought forth a new era of makeup. As the gaslights burned brighter, the makeup of the past looked more muted and dull to audiences. With this change in makeup, colors could be intensified.

Marketing Makeup

Ludwig Leichner developed a greasepaint and powder company in 1873. As both an opera singer and chemist, he was able to use his knowledge to develop a product that sold worldwide. He also developed pomatums, better known now as pomade, that gave color, shine, style, and scent to hair and wigs.

Stage to Screen

With the birth of film in the 1900s came added challenges for actors. To be believable on the big screen, makeup had to be subtler than on stage. Thick greasepaint applications were out. Actors had to find ways to apply their makeup subtly. **Typecasting** emerged in film. Directors cast roles by looking for actors who resembled the characters and required less makeup to make them believable.

STOP! THINK...

The first black-and-white motion pictures posed difficulties for designers. Look at the color wheels and answer these questions:

- ◎ What color would blue eyes appear on black-and-white film?

- ◎ Why do you think red fabric and makeup were not used during this time?

- ◎ Which shift from color to black and white is most surprising to you?

Time Line of Makeup History

The history of makeup in theater is closely related to the changing trends seen around the world. Take a look at how times have changed, and look closely for any signs of history repeating.

10,000 BC: Egyptians use oils and ointments to soften their skin. Perfumes are used in religious rituals.

4000 BC: Egyptian women use copper and lead minerals to line their eyes and **contour** their faces. Women begin to carry makeup in boxes.

3000 BC: Chinese women begin staining their fingernails with pigments. Deeper reds are reserved for the upper class.

1000 BC: Greeks whiten their faces with chalk or lead, and use red clay on their cheeks for blush and to stain their lips.

AD 300: Indians use henna to dye their hair and create designs on their skin for rituals.

1500: In England, red and blonde hair becomes *en vogue*. It is thought to create an angelic appearance. White lead paint is used to create a pale look.

1900: Zinc oxide is used as face powder, instead of more poisonous lead.

1930s: Hollywood films heavily influence the everyday makeup look.

1960s: One of the first brands marketed to teens is available.

1970s: The first cosmetic products aimed at African American women becomes widely available in the United States.

"Makeup" a Plan

Makeup design in a production requires careful planning. Many makeup artists work with costumers to come up with their looks. While the costumes must fit the actors' bodies, makeup must enhance the actors' faces. Before any of this work can begin, it is a good idea to get on the same page with the director about his or her vision.

Preparing

Planning for makeup for a production means looking closely at the needs of the characters and time period. A makeup designer also needs to consider the venue. Designing for a small theater versus a Broadway stage may change the products being used. The same character in both settings will look similar to the audience, but the methods of applying the makeup changes. Training in makeup design helps artists to understand these different techniques better.

It is important to create a schedule for makeup design. First, the actors' faces are photographed. Then, makeup is designed on a template. Next, trial runs of makeup application are done. Finally, the design for the production is completed. This schedule works best if deadlines are set. With these dates in mind, the designer can work toward these goals and share ideas with the director and other designers more clearly. Communication with the actors and production team during development is very important.

Key to Makeup Design

Pat McGrath, a leading makeup designer, says, "Creativity is your best makeup skill. Don't be afraid to experiment."

THINK LINK

◎ What would you want to know first from the director when designing the makeup for a show?

◎ What resources would you use to research the time period of a show?

◎ What questions would you ask of the lighting designer that would help you choose the makeup color palette?

Researching

Once the schedule is planned, it is time to start brainstorming and researching ideas for the production. The makeup designer should listen closely to the director and other designers but not be afraid to voice his or her own ideas. The designer's creative input might be the push others need. And, of course, a good designer's ideas can be supported by the research he or she has done.

Looking into the time period of the production is often the first step in planning makeup design. It is important to know makeup trends of the time. As the makeup designer looks into the world to be created, he or she can find inspiration in many places. Photography or art from the time period is a good place to start. Magazines, books, and other productions set in that same era help as well.

Sometimes makeup designers must create new worlds. When this happens, creativity is the guide. Taking inspiration from films, works of art, and the script will help guide the designer's process. Designers should be open to inspiration everywhere and should do research to be prepared for design meetings as early as possible. It may be useful for a designer to carry a sketchbook at all times. Clippings from magazines, images from the Internet, and ideas from nature can all be incorporated.

History Lessons

Fashion trends tend to repeat themselves every few decades. Being aware of the past can help to predict future trends and keep makeup designers on the cutting edge. Many successful designers begin with styles from the past and add their own twist.

Designing

After research, the next step is design. Templates and colors play key roles. Having a picture of the actor can help with makeup choice. It is also helpful for a makeup designer to speak to costume and lighting designers beforehand so that color choices are well informed.

With template and colored pencils in hand, the designer sketches the design for each character. The sketches should begin with the basic look and then have color added. Attaching pictures from the research can remind the designer of good color choices for the time period. The designer should also enhance the actor's natural coloring. Samples of the makeup colors, including brand and pigment names, should be added to the template.

When it's time for performances to start, the makeup designer decides who will apply the makeup. With difficult designs or close-up work, the designer might choose to do the work solo. If there are many actors in the cast, the designer might walk them through the template and application so they can do it themselves. Sometimes, a makeup team is brought together. Each member of the team becomes an expert on specific looks and is in charge of those actors throughout the production.

Under the Lights

Lighting has a big effect on makeup colors, so makeup designs need to be seen under the correct stage or film lighting before being finalized. For example, pink lighting makes warm colors more intense. Green lighting makes pale flesh colors and reds look washed out, and blue lighting causes flesh tones to appear red or purple.

STOP! THINK...

- ◎ How could a template help a makeup designer communicate with a director?
- ◎ How does the makeup design help to create the character?
- ◎ How might technology help with creating a makeup template?

face chart

Skin

Eyes

Lips

Tips and Tools of the Trade

A makeup designer must have a well-stocked makeup kit of foundations, brushes, powders, creams, and cleansers. Foundations, blushes, and shadows should be available for different skin tones and types. Liquids, creams, pencils, and powders work differently on every face. Experimenting with makeup ahead of time will allow the designer to see what works to create the desired looks.

Airbrushing

Many film designers focus on **airbrushing**. Airbrush makeup is applied with a machine that sprays liquid makeup onto the skin. The makeup flows out in a fine, even mist that blends easily. The makeup artist moves the airbrush back and forth less than a foot away from the skin.

Airbrushing was first used in 1959 on the set of *Ben Hur*. As the technique has improved, it has become more widespread. A flawless finish has become more needed with **high-definition** video. Airbrushing is now very popular on television sets.

Prime Time

Using a makeup **primer** can help to create the flawless coverage wanted for daily wear as well as close-ups in television and film. These products prepare the skin by filling in large pores or fine lines. Applying it can also help the makeup have a surface to stick to instead of seep into.

Face Painting

Some special makeup designs require face painting. Fantasy characters, animals, and wounds can be created using stage makeup in this way. It takes practice and time to develop the skills to blend and highlight. When done properly, the results are amazing.

Makeup Life

Since makeup is applied directly onto the skin, older makeup runs the risk of causing skin breakouts and infections. A general rule is that the closer it is to your eyes, the less time it should spend in the drawer. Also, if a product is the first layer of makeup against the skin, it should be tossed sooner. Powders usually are safe to keep for longer periods of time. If any makeup passes the two-year mark, it may be time to kiss it goodbye!

Hygiene

Taking care of makeup is important. Cleaning brushes and sponges will help to preserve the products safely. By far the most important element of makeup is having a blank canvas to apply the design. Actors and actresses must work to keep their skin clean and healthy. This helps makeup artists apply the products to achieve the desired look. Products used in theatrical makeup, like oil-based products, **spirit gums**, and latex can irritate the skin, as can harsh cleansers. To prevent irritation, actors should gently cleanse their skin before applying makeup and remove it thoroughly after every performance. Doing this will keep the skin in better condition.

Natural Cleansers

Using natural products to care for skin has made a comeback. Avocado, oatmeal, egg whites, and honey are all used in natural masks for hydration and toning. Coconut oil is a new trend in anti-bacterial washes and moisturizers.

Makeup Lifespan
Liquid vs. Powder

makeup	liquid/cream	powder/pencil
foundation	6 months	2 years
eyeliner	3 months	2 years
eye shadow	6 months	2 years
blush/bronzer	6–12 months	2 years

STOP! THINK...

This chart shows the shelf life for liquid/cream and powder/pencil makeup. Use the chart to answer the following questions:

◎ What types of makeup can be kept the longest?

◎ Why do you think creams have a shorter life than powders?

Skin Sensitivities

Designers always test a small amount of any new makeup, applying it on the inside of the wrist and waiting 24 to 48 hours for any reaction. If none appears, it's safe to use that product. Choosing makeup made for sensitive skin is good practice. Designers start with a moisturizer on clean skin, followed by eye makeup, and then face and cheek makeup. A loose mineral powder is used to reduce shine since it won't clog pores.

A designer must be aware of the actors' skin types. Skin sensitivity can be a warning sign of an actual **allergic reaction**. There are many common causes for skin reactions, and ingredients in makeup can irritate skin, too. Perfumes, chemicals, and natural plant-based materials can all cause problems. Latex used to create **prosthetics**, such as fake noses, chins, and ears is another irritant. There are substitutes for latex, depending on the designer's or actor's needs. Silicone rubber can be made into prosthetics, and makeup wax can be used for fake wounds. Spirit gum, an adhesive, can be used to attach hair and fake body parts.

Brush It Off

Makeup artists clean their brushes regularly. Natural-hair brushes are cleaned after each use and conditioned regularly. **Synthetic** brushes require different cleaners and don't need to be conditioned. All brushes should be dried on a towel on their side. Drying a brush with the bristles facing up will make the brush fall apart sooner.

Tin Man Trouble

In 1939's *The Wizard of Oz*, Buddy Ebsen was originally cast as the Tin Man but had an allergic reaction to the metals in the makeup they applied for screen tests. The aluminum dust landed him in the hospital in an oxygen tent when his lungs failed. He was replaced by Jack Haley, who wore a different mixture of makeup as a precaution.

Prosthetics

Special-effects makeup designers work to make the unimaginable happen. Zombies, vampires, mortal wounds, mystical creatures, and other makeup challenges are these artists' specialties. While some effects today are done with computer-generated images (CGI), the use of prosthetics is still common.

Prosthetic makeup had its beginnings in Greek masks. It became a studied art with the introduction of motion pictures. These makeup artists go beyond simply taking pictures of their actors. Instead, they do a process called lifecasting, which involves making molds of actors' faces. Plaster gauze or silicone rubber that is safe for the skin creates the **negative**. Once dried, it is filled with cement to make a **positive** form that the makeup designer can use.

Clay is used to build up parts of the face. Latex, false hair, wax, and netting can create textures and effects. Test runs are performed to make sure the actor isn't allergic to any of the materials. The director views and gives feedback at each step. Once the final design is agreed upon, a realistic-looking piece is made. Prosthetics are put on with spirit gum and taken off with a special remover. The process can take hours to complete every day.

Makeup Magic

The prosthetic makeup used for the movie *Mrs. Doubtfire* took four hours every day to create. It paid off in the end, though, as the film won the Academy Award® for Makeup in 1994.

1

2

prosthetic makeup
process

3

51

Let's Face It

Learning how to put on makeup is a rite of passage for many teenagers. Some teens learn about makeup simply to conceal blemishes. Others want to even out their complexions. And then, there are those who are gifted with true artistic skills. When such students find a theater program willing to put their talents to work, the fun can begin! Learning the basic steps of applying makeup will help aspiring designers reach their potentials.

Foundation

Before applying foundation, makeup artists first wash their hands with soap and warm water and dry them thoroughly. The artist first applies a primer to even out the actor's skin texture. Then she applies foundation using her fingertips, a foundation brush, makeup sponge, or airbrush. Each technique allows the makeup to fully cover the skin and provide an even skin tone for applying the rest of the design.

No Mixing!

To prevent contaminating makeup products, artists pour a little of the makeup onto a mirror or palette. They dip their brushes in distilled water to keep the colors separate, or they use different brushes for each product.

Getting Started

If makeup is new to you and you want to get started, here are some possible supplies for your first makeup kit: foundation, powder, light blush, neutral eye shadow, and mascara.

General Contouring

The makeup technique of contouring can bring out facial features that may need to be accented or can hide features that need to be downplayed. Artists also use contouring to bring unusual looking characters to life.

For contour color, the designer chooses a shade darker than the foundation color. The highlighter color should be about the same color as the foundation with a hint of shine.

To contour cheekbones, the designer has the actor suck in his or her cheeks and shades along and beneath the sunken area, and then the designer blends well with a finger or sponge. To slim a nose, the makeup artist blends two lines of the shading cream or powder from the brows down the sides of the nose.

Highlighting brings lights to certain areas of the face. Pat the highlighter up and down the cheekbones, and then dab a bit on the brow bones, the center of the chin, and the tip of the nose.

Aging an actor is done with contour makeup. Natural wrinkle lines already on the face are traced with a brown pencil or powder that darkens the creases. The creases are then highlighted with light pencil, and shadows are added around these lines. The makeup is blended and then set with powder.

Contouring is also combined with prosthetics and special effects to create fantasy creatures. It's amazing what a little light and shadow can do to create stunning and even terrifying effects!

Chalk It Up!

If you think the art of contouring is a modern technique, think again. In the mid-1500s, actors in Elizabethan England would apply chalk and soot to their faces so the audience could read their expressions more easily.

Bringing Characters to Life

Creating a new world for the stage and screen requires more than just great costumes and believable makeup. The talents of designers breathe new life into old classics. New plays become even more interesting with powerful visual elements. The work of a designer may finish for one show, but there will be a need for talented people to design as long as there are productions running.

Almost anyone can take the first steps toward becoming a designer. Whether sewing classes are needed or practice in applying makeup, if someone wants to learn to design, it's never too early to begin. Practice those new skills and find a place where you can learn from others who have more experience. Take pictures of interesting designs and keep these images in a portfolio. The combination of creativity and hard work might one day help you get a job designing on a production.

Never be afraid to get creative with designs. Thinking outside the box can revolutionize the industry. Just as airbrushing and prosthetics were dreamed up decades ago, there may be a new idea that will change the way designs are created moving forward.

Show Off

A collection of designs is called a portfolio. In it, a designer keeps copies of templates, renderings, and photographs of past productions. Today, portfolios may be archived on a website, but many professionals still carry paper copies for interviews.

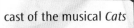
cast of the musical *Cats*

Glossary

airbrushing—the application of makeup through an air-released spray

allergic reaction—a body's negative physical response to a contaminant, such as plant matter or certain foods, characterized by symptoms such as skin rash, itching, sneezing, or restricted breathing

altered—changed, especially in regard to size but also in regard to design

archaeologists—scientists who study ancient cultures

artisans—skilled craftspersons

basting—a temporary stitch used to hold fabric together until it can permanently sewn.

body stockings—thin, one-piece, skin-tight garments that can be stuffed to create different body shapes for the wearer

britches—short pants, or trousers, fastened just below the knee

commedia dell'arte—Italian comedy of the sixteenth to eighteenth centuries improvised from common situations and stock characters

contour—shade and highlight to define the shape of a face

corset—a close-fitting undergarment tightened with lacing

costume plot—the plan for character costumes for a production

cravat—fabric, tie, or lace worn around the neck

embroidered—decorated with ornamental needlework

enhance—raise to a higher degree; improve

features—prominent characteristics or parts

gels—thin, colored sheets that can be placed in front of a light to change the light color onstage

high-definition—referring to a high degree of visual resolution, especially in film or video

mechanics—the details about how something works or is done

mimicked—imitated or copied

negative—a form or copy of the reverse or inverted image or model

notions—the items sewn onto a garment, such as snaps, buttons, and even thread

obi—a wide sash worn with a kimono

palettes—ranges of colors used by an artist

pantalets—frilled trim attached to the bottom of women's undergarments or skirts

pigments—substances that give things color

positive—a form or copy of the exact image or model

primer—makeup that goes directly on the skin and lays the foundation for a smooth application of all other makeup

production meeting—when producers and the creative team gather to talk

prosthetics—artificial structures applied to create illusions

realism—portrayals of stories and situations in a way that seems real to life

renderings—drawings or representations of planned designs

rituals—certain procedures for religious ceremonies

spirit gums—glues used to attach false hair or prosthetics to actors

suspension of disbelief—ability to let go of the reality they think they know

swatches—fabric samples

synthetic—composed of man-made materials

templates—patterns or models used for planning

touring companies—groups of performers who travel from city to city to perform plays

tunics—long, loose garments, usually sleeveless, originally worn by Greeks and Romans

typecasting—choosing actors based on their physical and personality traits

vintage—an object or piece of clothing from a past era

Index

Check It Out!

Books

Aucoin, Kevyn. 1999. *Making Faces*. Little, Brown and Company.

Blackwood, Gary. 2000. *The Shakespeare Stealer*. Perfection Learning.

Brown, Deni. 1996. *The Complete Book of Sewing: A Practical Step-by-Step Guide to Sewing Techniques*. Dorling Kinderslay Limited.

Eldridge, Lisa. 2015. *Face Paint: The Story of Makeup*. Harry N. Abrams.

Green, John, and David Levithan. 2010. *Will Grayson, Will Grayson*. Dutton Books for Young Readers.

Leventon, Melissa. 2008. *What People Wore When: A Complete Illustrated History of Costume from Ancient Times to the Nineteenth Century for Every Level of Society*. St. Martin's Griffin.

Websites

AllFreeSewing. *Free Patterns to Keep You in Stitches*. www.allfreesewing.com

Oscars. www.oscars.org